PIANO VOCAL GUITAR

Disney

CAMP ROCK 2
THE FINAL JAM

ISBN 978-1-4234-9386-0

WALT DISNEY MUSIC COMPANY, INC.
WONDERLAND MUSIC COMPANY

HAL•LEONARD® CORPORATION
7777 W. BLUEMOUND RD. P.O. BOX 13819 MILWAUKEE, WI 53213

In Australia Contact:
Hal Leonard Australia Pty. Ltd.
4 Lentara Court
Cheltenham, Victoria, 3192 Australia
Email: ausadmin@halleonard.com.au

Visit Hal Leonard Online at
www.halleonard.com

BRAND NEW DAY

Words and Music by KARA DioGUARDI
and MITCH ALLAN

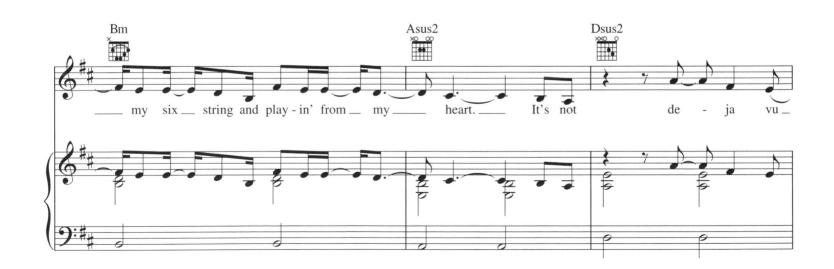

So dra - ma free. ___ I'm all a - bout ___

___ the mu - sic, I just wan - na sing. ___ Watch me

live out my dream. ___ I'm gon - na rock ___

D.S. al Coda

___ that stage ___ and give my ev - 'ry - thing. ___ I'm gon - na

FIRE

Words and Music by DAPO TORIMIRO
and LYRICA ANDERSON

Moderate Hip Hop

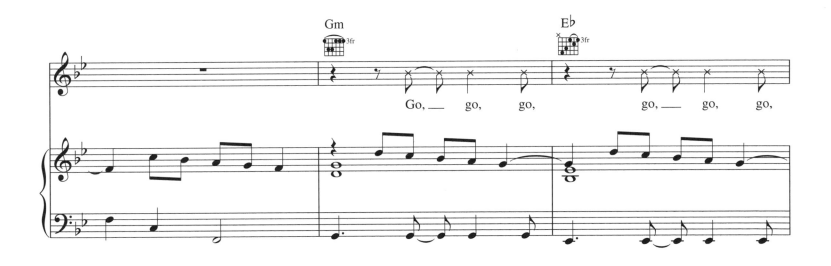

* Recorded a half step higher.

CAN'T BACK DOWN

Words and Music by TIM JAMES,
ANTONINA ARMATO and THOMAS STURGES

Moderately, with energy

We can't, we can't back down. We can't, we

can't back down. ___ We can't, we can't back down. ___

We can't, we can't back down. Not right now, we can't back down. ___

IT'S ON

Words and Music by TOBY GAD,
LYRICA ANDERSON and KOVASCIAR MYVETTE

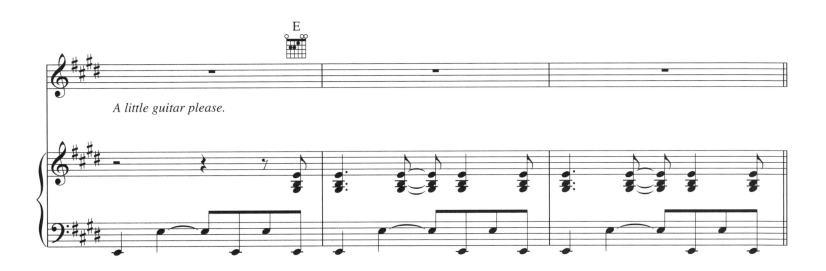

It's on, ___ it's on. ___ *(Ad lib lyrics.)*

Additional Lyrics

Rap: There, there, there, there... there is no competition, that's why we in the number one position.
     That crew can't hang with us. Man, we're too dangerous.
     Uh, uh, ain't got the style or the stamina. Just doin' my thing, get hooked on a swing.
     Rockin' the place, droppin' the bass. Makin' all the girls sing. Uh huh, yeah, we make the bells ring.

WOULDN'T CHANGE A THING

Words and Music by ADAM ANDERS,
NIKKI HASSMAN and PEER ASTROM

Female: It's like he does-n't hear a word I say. His mind is some-where far a-way and I don't know how to get there. It's

* *Recorded a half step higher.*

HEART & SOUL

Words and Music by TIM JAMES,
ANTONINA ARMATO, STEVE RUSHTON
and AARON DUDLEY

Moderate Rock

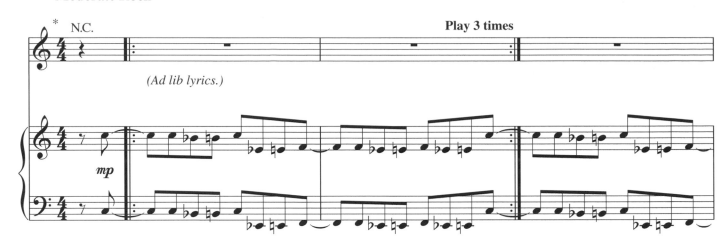

(Ad lib lyrics.)

mp

Play 3 times

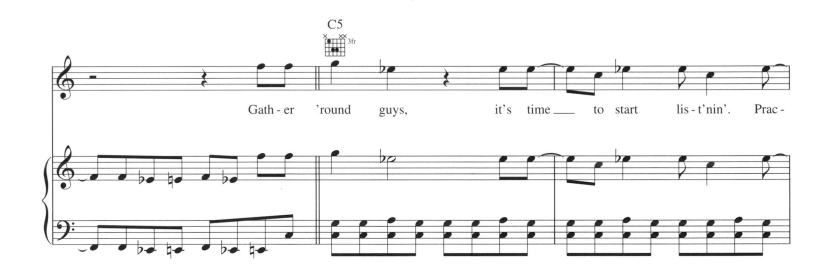

Gath - er 'round guys, it's time ___ to start lis - t'nin'. Prac -

- tice makes per - fect but per - fect's not work - in'. There's a lot more to mu - sic than

* Recorded a half step lower.

and __ soul __ you can rock __ and roll. __

You can rock __ and roll. __

(Instrumental solo ad lib.)

Spoken lyric: (See additional lyrics)

Additional Lyrics

Spoken: All right now, take it low.
Now I need the spotlight to hit me right here as the crowd starts to cheer.
I need the fan to blow right through my rock star hair, right here.

YOU'RE MY FAVORITE SONG

Words and Music by JEANNIE LURIE,
ARIS ARONCHITIS and CHEN NEEMAN

* *Recorded a half step lower.*

INTRODUCING ME

Words and Music by
JAMIE HOUSTON

I'm good at wastin' time. I think lyrics need to rhyme. And you're not askin' but I'm try'n' to grow a moustache. I eat cheese but only on pizza please and sometimes on a home-

* Recorded a half step lower.

TEAR IT DOWN

Words and Music by TOBY GAD,
LYRICA ANDERSON and KOVASCIAR MYVETTE

we own it. To-night we run it.

We gon' tear it down. Ahh,

ahh, ahh,

we gon' tear it down. Ahh,

Male rap: Yes, dem no want to contest we.

WHAT WE CAME HERE FOR

Words and Music by
JAMIE HOUSTON

THIS IS OUR SONG

Words and Music by ADAM WATTS
and ANDY DODD

Male: So, let's sing na, na, na, na, na, hey, ___ ya. Come on and sing na, na, na, na, na, hey, ___ ya.

Both: This is our song, that's ___ all that mat - ters 'cause we all be - long ___ right ___ here to - geth - er.

DIFFERENT SUMMERS

Words and Music by
JAMIE HOUSTON

Moderate Folk Rock

We're like a mel - o - dy __ with no __ words, __ un - til we fig - ure it __ out __

we sing la, la, la, la, __ la, la.

Cm

I hope you did ___ 'cause I ___ can tell ___ you _____

Db

that's some - thin' I'll nev - er for - get. __

Ab

Cb

D.S. al Coda

____ I won't __ for - get __ if

CODA

Abmaj7

start it all o - ver a - gain. _

Gb

Ab

Eb

On - ly friends _____ just be - gin - ning. _____ But I

Bbsus

Bb

Gb

Ab

hope that we find __ it a - gain ____ so _ we can _____ go _ from here, _

start it all ov - er a - gain. _____ A-

gain and a - gain ___ and a - gain ___ and a - gain. ___ A - gain ___

___ and a - gain ___ and a - gain. _____ Will

we re - mem - ber dif - f'rent sum - mers? _____

WALKIN' IN MY SHOES

Words and Music by JOACIM PERSSON,
NICLAS MOLINDER, JOHAN ALKENAS,
LYRICA ANDERSON and PAM SHEYNE

Recorded a half step higher.

on my feet, __ you'll be want - in' more, __ want - in' more, oh. __

D.S. al Coda

_____ *Both:* Oh, _____

CODA Gm

No one's gon - na lose walk - in' in my __ shoes.

Walk - in' in my __ shoes.

IT'S NOT TOO LATE

Words and Music by ADAM WATTS
and ANDY DODD